Guide to

I0012294

Practical Guide

V. Telman

Guide to Plesk

1.Introduction

Plesk is a web server management software that allows website administrators to easily and efficiently manage their servers. It is a control panel that offers a wide range of features to simplify the management of servers, websites, and applications.

The software was developed by Plesk International GmbH and is available for various platforms, including Linux and Windows. With its intuitive interface and powerful features, Plesk has become an essential tool for website administrators and hosting companies that manage a large number of servers.

One of Plesk's main features is its ability to manage both Linux and Windows servers. This makes it a versatile choice for those managing a variety of web servers. Additionally, Plesk offers a wide range of features for website management, including the ability to create and manage user accounts, manage databases, and install web applications.

Among Plesk's most popular features is SSL certificate management, which allows users to secure their websites with encrypted connections. Plesk also offers advanced features for website management, such as the ability to set access rules and protect websites from malicious attacks.

Another key feature of Plesk is its support for email services management. Users can easily configure email accounts, manage anti-spam filters, and monitor the performance of the mail server. This makes Plesk an ideal choice for businesses managing a large amount of email.

Additionally, Plesk offers a wide range of tools to facilitate server management, including an integrated backup system, pcrformance monitoring tools, and a resource management system to track server resource usage.

Finally, Plesk offers a wide range of extensions and plugins that allow users to customize the software to their needs. Administrators can easily extend Plesk's functionality by adding extensions for backup management, server security, content management, and much more.

Plesk is a comprehensive solution for web server management that offers businesses and website administrators a wide range of features to simplify and optimize server management. With its intuitive interface, powerful features, and customizable extensions, Plesk has established itself as one of the leading control panels for web server management.

2.Plesk Installation

The installation of Plesk is a relatively simple process that only requires a few steps. In this detailed guide, I will explain how to install Plesk on your server.

Before you begin, make sure you have everything you need to proceed with the installation. You will need a server running an operating system compatible with Plesk, such as CentOS, Debian, Ubuntu, or Windows Server. Make sure you also have access to the root account or an account with administrator privileges on the server.

Once you have verified that you have all the necessary requirements, you can begin with the installation of Plesk. Here are the steps to follow:

1. Download the Plesk installation package from the official website. You can choose

from different versions of Plesk depending on your needs and the operating system of your server.

2. Once you have downloaded the installation package, transfer it to your server using an FTP client or SCP.

3. Access your server using a remote terminal or SSH connection. Make sure you are logged in as the root user or with administrator privileges.

4. Navigate to the directory where you transferred the Plesk installation package and decompress it using the tar command. For example, if the package is called plesk.tar.gz, you can decompress it with the command tar -xvzf plesk.tar.gz.

5. Once you have decompressed the package, navigate to the created directory and find the Plesk installation file. It is usually called

installer.sh.

6. Run the Plesk installation file with the command ./installer.sh. This will start the Plesk installation process and guide you through the initial configuration.

7. During the installation, you will be asked for some basic information, such as the email address of the Plesk administrator, the login password, and server configuration options. Make sure you correctly enter all the required information.

8. Once the initial configuration is completed, the Plesk installation will proceed automatically. This process may take a few minutes, depending on your server's performance and Internet connection speed.

9. Once the Plesk installation is complete, you can access the management interface through your web browser. Enter the IP address of

your server followed by port number 8443 (e.g. https://ip_address:8443) to access Plesk.

10. Log in using the email address and password of the Plesk administrator that you configured during installation. Once logged in, you will be ready to start using Plesk to manage your server.

Plesk offers a wide range of management features and tools that will allow you to easily manage your server, create and manage websites, install applications, and much more. Be sure to explore all the available features to make the most of them.

Remember that it is important to always keep Plesk updated to ensure the security and optimal performance of your server. Make sure to regularly check for available updates and install them promptly.

With this detailed guide, you will be able to

install Plesk on your server smoothly and start enjoying all its powerful management features.

3.Plesk Configuration

With Plesk, you can manage websites, databases, emails, and other server resources in an easy and intuitive way.

The configuration of Plesk is a relatively simple process that requires just a few steps. Once the software is installed on the server, you can access the Plesk admin interface using a web browser and the server's IP address followed by ":8443".

Upon logging in, the Plesk admin interface will open, displaying the main dashboard with information about the server status, websites, and allocated resources. From here, you can navigate through different sections and configure various server options.

The first thing to do in the Plesk configuration is to log in with the administrator credentials and set a secure password to protect the account. It is also advisable to enable two-factor authentication to increase the security of the account.

After completing these initial steps, you can start configuring websites on the server. To do this, you need to add the domains you want to host on the server using the dedicated section of the Plesk control panel.

Once the domains are added, you can further configure them by setting hosting settings, such as the site's root directory, the PHP version to use, and other site-specific parameters.

Additionally, you can manage databases on the server using Plesk's database manager. From here, you can add new databases, create new users, and set access privileges for each database.

Regarding emails, you can manage email

accounts on the server using Plesk's email module. From here, you can add new email accounts, set space quotas, and send and receive emails directly from the Plesk control panel.

To enhance server security, you can configure firewall rules, install SSL certificates to encrypt communications, and set security policies to protect the server from cyber attacks.

Finally, you can configure backup settings to schedule and automate data backups on the server. It is important to regularly create backups of data to prevent the loss of important information in case of hardware failures or human errors.

Plesk configuration is a simple process that requires just a few steps and allows administrators to easily manage their web server. With Plesk, you can configure websites, databases, emails, and other server resources in an intuitive and secure manner. With its advanced features and intuitive user interface, Plesk is an ideal solution for efficiently and securely managing a web server.

4.Domain Management in Plesk

Plesk is a web hosting management platform that offers a wide range of functionalities to manage servers and websites. Among the various features offered by Plesk is domain management, which allows users to easily create and manage their domains within the Plesk environment.

When using Plesk to manage your domains, you can manage all aspects related to domains, such as domain registration, DNS management, creation of subdomains, management of aliases, and much more.

One of the first things to do to manage your domains in Plesk is domain registration. Typically, Plesk offers a convenient tool to register new domains directly from the control panel interface. Simply enter the desired domain name and follow the instructions to complete the registration process. Once the domain has been successfully registered, you can view and manage it within Plesk.

After registering a domain in Plesk, you can start configuring the DNS for that domain. DNS is essential to direct web traffic to the correct server and ensure that the website associated with the domain is accessible to users. In Plesk, you can modify the DNS records of the domain, add new records, create subdomains, and much more.

In addition to DNS management, in Plesk you can create subdomains to divide the main website into more specific sections. Subdomains are useful for organizing website content more efficiently and improving user experience. With Plesk, you can create new subdomains in just a few clicks and easily manage them through the control panel interface.

Another important feature offered by Plesk for domain management is the ability to create aliases for existing domains. Aliases are essentially alternative names for a domain and can be used to redirect traffic from one domain to another. With Plesk, you can create aliases for your domains quickly and easily.

In addition to creating aliases, in Plesk you can also manage advanced domain settings, such as security settings, FTP access, SSL, and much more. Plesk offers a wide range of options to customize domain settings based on each user's specific needs.

Finally, another feature to mention regarding domain management in Plesk is the ability to monitor domain performance through integrated monitoring. This feature allows users to monitor the performance of their domains and receive notifications in case of traffic spikes or other issues that could affect website performance.

Domain management in Plesk offers users a range of powerful and flexible tools to effectively and conveniently manage their domains. With Plesk, you can register new domains, manage DNS, create subdomains, manage aliases and advanced domain settings, monitor performance, and much more. With its intuitive interface and numerous features, Plesk is an ideal solution for domain management for those who want a comprehensive and user-friendly web hosting environment.

5.Website management in Plesk

Managing websites in Plesk is a fundamental process for those who handle multiple websites on a server. Plesk is a web control panel that offers a wide range of tools and functionalities to simplify website management, allowing users to monitor server resources, configure website settings, manage user accounts, and much more.

One of the most important aspects of website management in Plesk is the creation and management of the websites themselves. With Plesk, users can create new websites in a few simple steps, assigning them space on the server, configuring domain names, and setting file and folder permissions. Additionally, users can efficiently manage multiple websites within Plesk, organizing them and allowing administrators to keep track of all their sites in one place.

Another essential feature of Plesk is database

management. With Plesk, users can create new databases, import and export data, and manage database users and privileges. This is particularly important for dynamic websites that use databases to store information such as content, users, and transactions.

File management is another critical area of website management in Plesk. Users can upload and download files, modify file and folder permissions, and view file logs to track all activities on the server. Additionally, users can create file backups and easily restore websites in case of problems.

Security is another priority in website management in Plesk. Users can configure website security settings such as SSL/TLS, DDoS protection, firewall, and authentication to protect the site from external threats and attacks. Additionally, users can monitor site integrity and receive real-time notifications in case of security issues.

Managing domains and user accounts is also a fundamental part of website management in Plesk. Administrators can register new domain names, configure DNS records, create and manage user accounts, and assign specific permissions for access to websites and server resources.

With Plesk, users can also manage server resources such as memory, bandwidth, and CPU to ensure websites operate efficiently and smoothly. Administrators can monitor server resources in real-time and receive notifications in case of overload or performance issues.

Finally, website management in Plesk also includes the ability to manage emails. Users can create new email accounts, configure email settings, filter spam, and monitor incoming and outgoing email traffic. This is particularly important for websites that use email for communication with customers and users.

Website management in Plesk is a complex process that requires technical skills and specific knowledge. However, with the numerous features and tools offered by Plesk, administrators can easily manage all their websites in one place, ensuring optimal performance, security, and user experience. If you use Plesk for website management, make sure to fully utilize all its features to optimize the management of your websites and enhance user experience.

6. Database management in Plesk

Plesk is a server management platform that offers a wide range of features to manage and configure databases. In particular, we focus on the management of databases in Plesk, which is an essential part for many websites and applications.

To get started, you need to access the Plesk control panel and navigate to the "Database" section. Here you can create new databases, manage users, and access administration tools for each database.

One of the first things to do is to create a new database. This can be done by clicking the "Add database" button and entering the database name, password, and selecting the desired database type (such as MySQL or PostgreSQL). Once the database is created, you can create tables and populate it with the necessary data.

After creating the database, you can add users who will have access to the database. You can create new users and assign them specific privileges to access and manage the database. For example, you can grant a user permission to run queries on the database, but not to modify the table structure.

Once the database and users are created, you can access administration tools for the database. In Plesk, you can use tools like phpMyAdmin to run SQL queries directly on the database, manage tables, and perform maintenance operations such as table optimization and data backup.

Another useful feature offered by Plesk is the ability to easily backup and restore databases. You can schedule regular backups of databases and restore data in case of accidental loss or server failure.

Additionally, Plesk offers the ability to monitor database performance to ensure they are running properly and without issues. You can monitor database resource usage, slowest queries, and errors that may occur when accessing data.

Finally, Plesk offers advanced database security features. You can set database access rules to ensure that only authorized users can access sensitive data. Additionally, you can encrypt sensitive data within the database to protect them from unauthorized access.

Database management in Plesk provides a range of essential features for creating, managing, and securing databases used for websites and applications. With the ability to create new databases, manage users, run SQL queries, and monitor performance, Plesk is a comprehensive solution for managing databases on web servers.

7.Email management in Plesk

Email management in Plesk is a fundamental operation to ensure that email communication within a server is efficient and secure. Plesk is a hosting management platform that allows you to control various server functionalities, including managing email mailboxes.

To manage emails in Plesk, you need to access the platform's administration interface. Once logged in, you can view and manage all email mailboxes on the server. Through the Plesk interface, you can create new email mailboxes, modify existing mailbox settings, set up anti-spam and anti-virus filters, back up emails, and manage distribution lists.

Creating a new email mailbox in Plesk is a simple and quick operation. Simply select the "Add email address" option from the email management interface and enter the desired address. You can also configure other parameters such as mailbox size, activation of anti-spam and anti-virus filters, managing aliases, and setting up automatic responses.

Existing mailbox settings can be easily modified through the Plesk interface. You can update the mailbox password, change the maximum mailbox size, enable or disable email storage, set up custom filters, and much more. Additionally, you can set up email forwarding to another email address to ensure all communications are received correctly.

To protect mailboxes from spam and viruses, Plesk offers the ability to activate anti-spam and anti-virus filters. These filters can be configured by the server administrator and set up based on the server's specific needs. Anti-spam and anti-virus filters help reduce the risk of receiving harmful or unwanted emails and ensure that mailboxes remain secure.

To ensure communication continuity, regularly backing up emails on the server is essential. Plesk offers the ability to back up email mailboxes quickly and easily, ensuring the security and integrity of emails. You can schedule automatic email backups or perform them manually at any time.

Distribution lists are another important feature offered by Plesk to efficiently manage emails. Distribution lists allow you to send communications to a group of recipients without having to manually enter each individual email address. You can create custom distribution lists and easily manage them through the Plesk interface.

Email management in Plesk is a fundamental operation to ensure that email communication within a server is efficient and secure. Through the Plesk administration interface, you can create new email mailboxes, modify existing mailbox settings, activate anti-spam and anti-virus filters, back up emails, and manage distribution lists quickly and easily. Thanks to the powerful features offered by Plesk, you can manage emails efficiently and ensure that all communications occur safely and reliably.

8.Managing files in Plesk

Plesk is a web server management platform that offers a wide range of features to help system administrators efficiently manage their servers. One of these features is file management, which allows users to upload, download, edit, and organize files on the server.

To access file management in Plesk, users can use the browser-based web interface that provides a wide range of tools and options for manipulating files. Once logged into Plesk, users can find the "File Manager" icon on the main screen, which allows access to the section dedicated to file management.

Within Plesk's File Manager, users can navigate through folders and files on the server, viewing detailed information about each element such as size, modification date, and access permissions. Additionally, users can upload new files, create new folders, rename or delete existing files, and modify access permissions.

One of the most useful features of Plesk's File Manager is the ability to directly edit server configuration files, such as .htaccess files for Apache or web.config files for IIS. This allows system administrators to easily make necessary changes to server configuration without having to use an external text editor.

Moreover, Plesk's File Manager also offers a preview option to view the content of files directly in the web interface, allowing users to quickly check the content of files without having to download them to their computer.

To ensure file security, Plesk supports SSL encryption to ensure secure data transmission between the user's browser and the server. Additionally, specific access permissions can be set to protect sensitive files from unauthorized access.

Other useful tools available in Plesk's file management include the ability to create and restore file and folder backups, synchronize files with cloud storage services like Dropbox or Google Drive, and advanced search capabilities to quickly find desired files.

File management in Plesk provides system administrators with an intuitive and powerful way to manage files and folders on the web server, allowing them to work efficiently and securely. With the advanced features and ease of use offered by Plesk, file management can be done efficiently while ensuring data security on the server.

9.Security in Plesk

Plesk is a web hosting management platform that offers a wide range of features to help users easily manage their websites and servers. However, security is a fundamental aspect to consider when using Plesk, as websites are often exposed to various online risks and threats.

To ensure the security of websites hosted on Plesk, it is crucial to adopt good security practices and properly configure the server. In this article, we will delve into the different aspects of security in Plesk and provide tips on how to protect your websites from potential threats and attacks.

1. Regular software updates: One of the key steps to ensure server security is to consistently keep the software updated. Make sure to regularly install updates for Plesk and all components and plugins used on the server. Updates often include bug fixes and security

patches that are essential to protect the server from known vulnerabilities.

2. Secure passwords: Passwords are the first line of defense against cyber attacks. Be sure to use secure and complex passwords for all user and administrative accounts on Plesk. Use a combination of uppercase and lowercase letters, numbers, and special characters, and ensure that passwords are long and not easily guessable. Additionally, it is advisable to regularly change passwords to ensure an added level of security.

3. Firewall: Implementing a firewall on the server can help protect it from cyber attacks and unauthorized intrusions. Plesk offers an integrated firewall that allows you to control and regulate inbound and outbound network traffic. Configure the firewall to block unauthorized traffic and only allow necessary connections for the server and websites hosted on it to operate.

4. SSL certificate: Using an SSL certificate is crucial to protect sensitive data transmitted between the server and website visitors. Make sure to properly configure an SSL certificate for each website hosted on Plesk and enable HTTPS connection to ensure secure data transmission. Additionally, it is advisable to use a valid and reliable SSL certificate to ensure maximum protection.

5. Anti-malware and antivirus protection: The presence of malware and viruses can compromise server security and harm websites hosted on it. To protect the server from cyber threats, it is advisable to install anti-malware and antivirus software on the server and configure it to regularly scan the system and files to detect and remove any threats. Be sure to always keep the anti-malware software updated to ensure effective protection against the latest threats.

6. Regular backups: Creating regular backups of websites is essential to ensure data recoverability in case of loss or file damage.

Use Plesk's built-in backup feature to create backups of websites and set up an automatic backup program to regularly perform backups and store them in a secure external location. In case of data loss, you can easily restore websites from a recent backup and minimize the risk of critical data loss.

7. Security monitoring: Constantly monitoring server and website security is crucial to promptly detect potential threats and cyber attacks. Use security monitoring tools to check network traffic, server activities, and system vulnerabilities, and take prompt action in case of suspicious behavior or potential threats. Additionally, it is advisable to set up security notifications to be immediately alerted in case of abnormal activities or unauthorized access attempts.

8. Access limitation: Limiting access to the server and websites only to authorized users is an important security measure to protect sensitive data and prevent unauthorized access. Use Plesk's access control features to

configure roles and privileges for users and assign specific levels of access based on their responsibilities. Additionally, it is advisable to deactivate or remove unnecessary user accounts and set access rules to limit access to the server and sensitive data only to authorized individuals.

Security in Plesk is a critical aspect to consider to protect websites and sensitive data hosted on the server. By adopting good security practices, properly configuring the server, and using advanced protection tools and measures, it is possible to ensure effective protection against cyber threats and maintain website security. By following the above tips and consistently keeping security measures up to date, you can minimize the risk of vulnerabilities and protect websites from potential cyber attacks.

10. Remote access to Plesk

To remotely access Plesk, it is possible to use different methods and tools based on the user's needs and preferences. In this article, we will describe the main methodologies for remotely accessing Plesk, specifically using different platforms and tools.

Before delving into the details of how to remotely access Plesk, it is important to understand what Plesk is exactly and what its main features are. Plesk is a web hosting management platform that allows users to manage websites, servers, and applications easily and efficiently. Among the main features of Plesk are domain management, website management, database management, email management, and much more.

Plesk offers the ability to access its dashboard remotely through various methods and tools, which can vary depending on the server configuration and user preferences. Below, we will describe some of the main methodologies for remotely accessing Plesk.

Remote access to Plesk via Plesk Control Panel

The most common and conventional way to remotely access Plesk is through the Plesk Control Panel, which is the web-based graphical interface for managing Plesk. To access Plesk through the Plesk Control Panel, simply open a web browser and enter the Plesk access URL in the following format: https://IPAddress:port, where "IPAddress" represents the server's IP address where Plesk is installed and "port" represents the port for accessing the Plesk Control Panel (usually the default port is 8443).

After entering the Plesk access URL, the Plesk Control Panel login page will appear, where you will need to enter the login credentials (username and password) to access the Plesk dashboard. Once logged in successfully, you can manage all of Plesk's features easily and intuitively directly from the web browser.

Remote access to Plesk via SSH

Another way to remotely access Plesk is through SSH (Secure Shell), which is a secure network protocol for establishing a secure and encrypted connection between a client and a server. To access Plesk via SSH, you need to use an SSH client such as PuTTY (for Windows) or Terminal (for macOS and Linux) and enter the server's IP address and login credentials (username and password) to access the server.

Once connected to the server via SSH, you can use command-line commands to manage and configure the server, including Plesk services. For example, you can use the "plesk login" command to access the Plesk Control Panel directly from SSH. This method is useful for experienced users who prefer to use the command line to access and manage Plesk.

Remote access to Plesk via FTP

Another way to remotely access Plesk is through FTP (File Transfer Protocol), which is a network protocol used to transfer files between a client and a server quickly and efficiently. To access Plesk via FTP, you need to use an FTP client like FileZilla or Cyberduck and enter the server's IP address, username, and password to access the server.

Once connected to the server via FTP, you can navigate through the server's directories and transfer files to and from the server easily and quickly. Although FTP access is primarily used for file transfer, you can also use these connections to perform other Plesk management operations.

Remote access to Plesk via API

Finally, another way to remotely access Plesk is through API (Application Programming

Interface), which is a set of procedures and protocols that allow different applications to communicate and interact with each other in an automated and programmable way. Plesk offers a comprehensive and documented API that allows developers to integrate and automate various Plesk management operations.

Using Plesk's API, you can create custom scripts and applications to automate operations such as account creation, domain management, service configuration, and much more. Plesk's API offers a more advanced and flexible approach to accessing and managing Plesk remotely and can be used by both experienced users and developers who want to create custom solutions for Plesk.

There are several methods to remotely access Plesk, each offering specific advantages and functionalities based on the user's needs. Whether accessing through the Plesk Control Panel, SSH, FTP, or API, it is important to choose the most suitable method for your needs and preferences to efficiently and securely manage your server and web resources.

11. Backup and Restore in Plesk

Plesk is a hosting management platform that allows users to easily manage their websites, applications, and hosting services. Among the many features offered by Plesk, one of the most important is certainly backup and restore of data.

Backup and restore of data are fundamental procedures to ensure the security and integrity of website and application data. In case of data loss due to human errors, malware, hardware failures, or other issues, it is essential to be able to quickly restore the data from the backup.

Plesk offers a very flexible and powerful backup and restore system that allows users to schedule regular backups, configure storage options, and easily restore data when needed.

To back up data in Plesk, users can use the

built-in backup module in the control panel. The backup module allows users to select files to include in the backup, choose the backup frequency, and configure storage options.

Users can back up website files and directories, MySQL databases, and mailboxes. It is also possible to set the number of backup copies to retain and choose the backup frequency, such as daily, weekly, or monthly.

Once the backup is configured, users can run it manually or schedule it to run automatically according to the specified settings. Backups can be stored locally on the server, on a remote server via FTP, or on a cloud service like Google Drive, Dropbox, or Amazon S3.

In case of data loss, users can easily restore data from the backup using Plesk's restore module. The restore module allows users to select the desired backup file, choose which data to restore, and initiate the restore process.

During the restoration process, users can choose to overwrite existing data with the data from the backup or restore the data to a new location. It is also possible to select individual files or directories to restore instead of restoring the entire backup.

Plesk also offers the option to restore data directly from the control panel without having to use the restore module. This option is particularly useful for quickly restoring specific files or databases without having to restore the entire backup.

Thanks to its powerful backup and restore functionality, Plesk allows users to protect their data and quickly restore it in case of loss. By being able to perform regular backups and configure storage options, users can be confident that their data is safe and protected from potential losses.

Backup and restore of data are fundamental procedures to ensure the security and integrity of website and application data. With Plesk's backup and restore system, users can protect their data and quickly restore it when needed. Thanks to its flexibility and power, Plesk offers users the peace of mind that their data is safe and protected from potential losses.

12.Monitoring and Reporting in Plesk

Plesk is a hosting management platform that offers numerous useful tools for monitoring and managing your servers. Among these tools, monitoring and reporting play a fundamental role in ensuring the security and proper functioning of the hosting services offered.

Monitoring allows you to keep track of various server parameters, such as storage capacity, bandwidth usage, CPU and memory usage, network traffic, and more. Thanks to this data, it is possible to identify any problems or overloads and intervene promptly to ensure the continuity of the service.

Plesk offers dedicated tools for monitoring, such as Plesk Health Monitor, which allows you to view the real-time health status of the server and the services running on it. Health Monitor provides detailed information on server workloads and resources used, allowing you to identify any stress or overload situations.

Moreover, you can configure alerts and notifications to be promptly notified in case of problems or anomalies. Thanks to these notifications, you can intervene promptly to resolve issues and ensure the availability of services.

In addition to real-time monitoring, it is also essential to analyze historical data to identify any trends and plan preventive interventions. Plesk offers advanced reporting tools that allow you to generate detailed reports on server and service performance. These reports allow you to monitor the trend over time of the main parameters, identify any critical issues, and plan corrective or improvement actions.

Thanks to reporting, you can thoroughly analyze the performance of the server and various services, identify any overload or inefficiency situations, and optimize the available resources. Furthermore, reports can also be useful for monitoring compliance with agreed service levels with clients and ensuring the quality of services offered.

To configure and customize monitoring and reporting in Plesk, you can use the Plesk Extension Catalog, which offers numerous plugins and extensions to expand the platform's functionalities. Among the available extensions are tools for advanced server monitoring, generating customized reports, and integrating with other monitoring and management systems.

Monitoring and reporting are two essential features to ensure the security and proper functioning of servers and hosting services. Thanks to advanced tools like those offered by Plesk, you can monitor server performance, promptly identify any problems, and optimize available resources to ensure the continuity of the service and customer satisfaction.

13.Customization and extensions in Plesk

Thanks to its intuitive and user-friendly interface, Plesk allows users to easily configure and manage their servers without the need for extensive technical knowledge.

One of the key features of Plesk is the ability to customize your hosting environment with extensions. Extensions are additional plugins that add extra functionality to the base software, allowing users to add new features and services to their server.

Extensions can be downloaded directly from the Plesk marketplace, which offers a wide range of options for customizing your hosting environment. Among the most popular extensions are advanced security tools like firewalls and antivirus, automatic backup tools, performance monitoring services, and much more. Once the desired extensions are installed, users can easily manage them through the Plesk interface, which offers options to activate, deactivate, and configure extensions according to their needs.

Additionally, Plesk offers the ability to customize the look and functionality of the interface itself. Users can customize their control panel by adding new widgets, changing colors and layout schemes, and even creating their own custom themes.

Customizing the Plesk interface allows users to create a more intuitive and efficient working environment by adapting the software to their specific needs. This improves the user experience and increases productivity in managing their server.

In addition to interface customization, users can extend the functionality of Plesk using APIs and SDKs. These tools allow developers to integrate Plesk with other platforms and services, creating custom solutions and extending the capabilities of the base software.

By using Plesk's APIs and SDKs, users can create custom applications, automate repetitive tasks, and integrate the software with other tools and services used by the user.

Customization and extensions in Plesk provide users with flexibility and the ability to adapt the software to their specific needs. With a wide range of available extensions, the ability to customize the interface, and the use of APIs and SDKs, users can create a personalized hosting environment and optimize the management of their web server.

14.Performance optimization in Plesk

Plesk is a web server management platform that provides users with a user-friendly interface to manage their websites, applications, and hosting services. An essential aspect to ensure a great user experience is optimizing the performance of the server where Plesk is installed.

Server performance optimization is a complex process that involves various practices and tools to maximize efficiency, speed, and stability. In this article, we will examine some key strategies to optimize performance in Plesk.

1. Update server and software: one of the first things to do to optimize server performance is to ensure that all software and operating system components are updated to the latest version. Updates often contain performance improvements and bug fixes that can help optimize the overall server performance.

In Plesk, you can manage operating system and software updates directly from the user interface using the automatic update tool. Additionally, it is advisable to configure the operating system to automatically run updates to ensure that the server is always up to date and secure.

2. Optimize web server settings: another important strategy to optimize performance in Plesk is to optimize web server settings. For example, you can configure the web server (like Apache, Nginx, or LiteSpeed) to use fewer resources and handle more requests more efficiently.

In Plesk, you can configure web server settings from the user interface by changing parameters such as maximum file upload size, web server cache, maximum number of connections, and so on. These settings can be adjusted based on the specific needs of the server and hosted websites.

3. Optimize database settings: another critical area to optimize performance in Plesk is the database. The database is responsible for storing and accessing data from websites and applications, so it is essential to optimize its performance to ensure optimal speed and stability of the server.

In Plesk, you can manage the database directly from the user interface using tools like phpMyAdmin or Adminer. You can optimize database performance by setting indexes for tables, reducing the number of complex queries, and using cache for frequent queries.

4. Use cache to improve performance: caching is an effective strategy to improve web server performance. Cache temporarily saves resources (like files, data, images) on a server so they can be quickly retrieved when needed, rather than recalculated from scratch every time.

In Plesk, you can configure cache using

extensions like LiteSpeed Cache, Redis, or Varnish Cache. These extensions allow you to cache server resources to improve performance and reduce webpage loading times.

5. Performance monitoring: finally, it is important to constantly monitor server performance to identify any issues and take timely action to resolve them. In Plesk, you can use the performance monitoring tool to track key parameters like CPU usage, memory, network traffic, and so on.

Performance monitoring can help identify any bottlenecks or configuration issues affecting server performance. Proper and timely analysis of monitoring data can help take corrective measures and improve overall server performance.

Performance optimization in Plesk is an ongoing process that requires a combination of strategies and tools to maximize efficiency, speed, and stability. By following the practices described in this article and constantly monitoring server performance, you can ensure that websites and applications hosted on Plesk provide an optimal user experience.

15.Performance optimization in Plesk

Plesk is a web server management platform that provides users with a user-friendly interface to manage their websites, applications, and hosting services. An essential aspect to ensure a great user experience is optimizing the performance of the server where Plesk is installed.

Server performance optimization is a complex process that involves various practices and tools to maximize efficiency, speed, and stability. In this article, we will examine some key strategies to optimize performance in Plesk.

1. Update server and software: one of the first things to do to optimize server performance is to ensure that all software and operating system components are updated to the latest version. Updates often contain performance improvements and bug fixes that can help optimize the overall server performance.

In Plesk, you can manage operating system and software updates directly from the user interface using the automatic update tool. Additionally, it is advisable to configure the operating system to automatically run updates to ensure that the server is always up to date and secure.

2. Optimize web server settings: another important strategy to optimize performance in Plesk is to optimize web server settings. For example, you can configure the web server (like Apache, Nginx, or LiteSpeed) to use fewer resources and handle more requests more efficiently.

In Plesk, you can configure web server settings from the user interface by changing parameters such as maximum file upload size, web server cache, maximum number of connections, and so on. These settings can be adjusted based on the specific needs of the server and hosted websites.

3. Optimize database settings: another critical area to optimize performance in Plesk is the database. The database is responsible for storing and accessing data from websites and applications, so it is essential to optimize its performance to ensure optimal speed and stability of the server.

In Plesk, you can manage the database directly from the user interface using tools like phpMyAdmin or Adminer. You can optimize database performance by setting indexes for tables, reducing the number of complex queries, and using cache for frequent queries.

4. Use cache to improve performance: caching is an effective strategy to improve web server performance. Cache temporarily saves resources (like files, data, images) on a server so they can be quickly retrieved when needed, rather than recalculated from scratch every time.

In Plesk, you can configure cache using

extensions like LiteSpeed Cache, Redis, or Varnish Cache. These extensions allow you to cache server resources to improve performance and reduce webpage loading times.

5. Performance monitoring: finally, it is important to constantly monitor server performance to identify any issues and take timely action to resolve them. In Plesk, you can use the performance monitoring tool to track key parameters like CPU usage, memory, network traffic, and so on.

Performance monitoring can help identify any bottlenecks or configuration issues affecting server performance. Proper and timely analysis of monitoring data can help take corrective measures and improve overall server performance.

Performance optimization in Plesk is an ongoing process that requires a combination of strategies and tools to maximize efficiency, speed, and stability. By following the practices described in this article and constantly monitoring server performance, you can ensure that websites and applications hosted on Plesk provide an optimal user experience.

16. Development and Debugging Tools in Plesk

Plesk offers a wide range of tools to facilitate website development and debugging. Among these tools are specific debugging tools that allow developers to easily identify and resolve any coding errors or issues.

One of the main development and debugging tools offered by Plesk is the integrated debugger. This tool allows developers to pause code execution at any point and examine the state of variables and objects at that moment. This way, it is possible to quickly identify and correct any logic errors in the code.

Another useful tool is the server monitor, which provides detailed information about server resources such as CPU, memory, and disk space usage. This tool allows developers to identify any server performance issues and optimize available resources to ensure an optimal user experience.

Plesk also offers tools for database management, including phpMyAdmin and phpPgAdmin, which allow developers to easily access and manage databases associated with their websites. These tools provide an intuitive graphical interface for running queries, viewing and editing data in databases, making development and debugging work easier.

Regarding frontend debugging, Plesk offers tools such as element inspection and the JavaScript console, allowing developers to easily identify and resolve markup and JavaScript code errors on their websites. These tools provide advanced functionality for frontend code analysis and debugging, enabling developers to optimize performance and compatibility of their websites on different platforms and devices.

Moreover, Plesk offers advanced monitoring

and logging tools that enable developers to track visitor activities and behaviors on their websites. These tools provide detailed information on server requests, page loading times, HTTP responses, and more, allowing developers to easily identify and resolve performance or security issues.

Finally, Plesk offers file and directory management tools that allow developers to perform upload, download, and file management operations directly from the management interface. These tools significantly simplify the development and debugging process, enabling developers to work more efficiently and productively.

Plesk offers a wide range of development and debugging tools that simplify and optimize the website development process. With these tools, developers can quickly identify and resolve any coding errors or issues, ensuring an optimal user experience and improving the performance and security of their websites.

17. Automation of activities in Plesk

Plesk is a hosting management platform that offers a wide range of features to simplify and automate tasks related to server and website management. With its intuitive interface and powerful features, Plesk allows users to easily manage their servers, websites, applications, and more.

Automation of activities in Plesk is a very useful option to optimize time and simplify the work of server administrators and web developers. Through automation, it is possible to reduce human errors, increase efficiency, and improve overall productivity.

One of the main automation features in Plesk is the ability to create custom automation scripts using shell scripting language. These scripts allow users to automate a wide range of tasks, such as managing backups, installing new applications, configuring network services, and much more.

Additionally, Plesk offers a set of predefined automation tools that can be used to automate many common tasks related to server and website management. For example, you can automate the process of installing and configuring popular applications like WordPress, Joomla, Drupal, and Magento using Plesk's automatic installation tools.

Plesk also offers the ability to schedule recurring tasks using the integrated scheduling program. This tool allows users to create and schedule automation scripts to perform specific tasks at specific times. For example, you can schedule an automatic daily backup of the website or run regular server security checks.

Another useful automation feature in Plesk is the ability to configure automation rules to monitor and automatically manage server resources. For example, you can configure automation rules to automatically resize server resources based on server workload or to automatically start new server instances in case of traffic spikes.

Furthermore, Plesk offers a wide range of extensions and plugins that allow users to further extend and customize the platform's automation capabilities. These extensions can be used to integrate Plesk with other automation tools and services, create custom workflows, and much more.

Thanks to its powerful suite of automation tools and intuitive interface, Plesk is the ideal choice for server administrators and web developers looking to simplify and optimize their server and website management tasks. With Plesk, you can easily automate a wide range of tasks and improve the overall efficiency of hosting management.

18. Plesk Glossary

To fully understand how Plesk works, it is useful to know some technical terms and key concepts that are used within the platform. Below, a detailed glossary of some of the most common terms used in Plesk will be provided.

1. Control panel: The control panel is the web interface through which you can manage and configure the server and websites on Plesk. Through the control panel, you can control all the features of Plesk, including website management, databases, emails, and server settings.

2. Web server: A web server is a software that allows you to host and distribute websites on the internet. Plesk includes an integrated web server that allows you to host websites on a server managed with Plesk.

3. Hosting: The term hosting refers to the practice of hosting websites on a server that can be accessed from the internet. Plesk offers hosting features that allow you to host and manage websites on a server with Plesk.

4. Domain: A domain is a unique web address used to identify a website on the internet. Plesk allows you to manage and configure the domains of websites hosted on a server with Plesk.

5. Subdomain: A subdomain is an additional domain that can be used to create separate sections or web pages within a main domain. Plesk allows you to manage and configure subdomains for websites hosted on a server with Plesk.

6. DNS: The Domain Name System is a system that translates server IP addresses into domain names readable by users. Plesk includes an integrated DNS service that allows you to manage and configure DNS records for

domains hosted on a server with Plesk.

7. SSL certificate: An SSL (Secure Sockets Layer) certificate is a security protocol that allows for an encrypted connection between the server and the user's browser. Plesk offers SSL certificate management features that allow you to install, configure, and manage SSL certificates for websites hosted on a server with Plesk.

8. Database: A database is a data management system that allows you to store and retrieve information in a structured way. Plesk supports various types of databases, including MySQL and PostgreSQL, and allows you to manage and configure databases for websites hosted on a server with Plesk.

9. Email: Plesk includes email management features that allow you to configure and manage email accounts for domains hosted on a server with Plesk. Through Plesk, you can create new email accounts, configure anti-

spam and antivirus filters, and manage email
sending and receiving settings.

10. Backup: Plesk includes backup features
that allow you to create backups of websites,
databases, and server settings. Backups can be
scheduled to run automatically at regular
intervals and can be restored in case of data
loss.

11. FTP: File Transfer Protocol is a network
protocol used to transfer files between a client
and a server. Plesk includes FTP features that
allow you to configure and manage FTP
accounts to enable file transfers to and from
the server.

12. Extensions: Plesk offers an extensions
system that allows you to add additional
features to the control panel. Extensions can
include new features, custom themes,
integrations with external services, and much
more.

13. Firewall: A firewall is a security system that monitors and controls incoming and outgoing network traffic from the server. Plesk includes an integrated firewall that allows you to protect the server from network attacks and unauthorized intrusions.

14. Cache: Cache is a temporary memory used to store frequently accessed data in order to speed up the loading time of web pages. Plesk includes caching features that allow you to optimize the performance of websites hosted on a server with Plesk.

15. WordPress Toolkit: WordPress Toolkit is a Plesk extension that allows you to manage and configure WordPress-based websites. With WordPress Toolkit, you can quickly and easily install, update, copy, and migrate WordPress sites.

16. Git: Git is a version control system used to manage the source code of software projects. Plesk includes Git integration features that

allow you to manage Git repositories directly from the control panel.

17. Docker: Docker is a platform for managing virtualized containers used to deploy and manage applications in isolation. Plesk includes Docker integration features that allow you to manage Docker containers directly from the control panel.

18. Ruby on Rails: Ruby on Rails is a web development framework used to create dynamic and interactive web applications. Plesk supports Ruby on Rails and allows you to configure and manage Ruby on Rails applications on a server with Plesk.

19. Node.js: Node.js is a runtime environment that allows you to run server-side JavaScript code. Plesk supports Node.js and allows you to configure and manage Node.js applications on a server with Plesk.

20. Dedicated server: A dedicated server is a physical server reserved exclusively for a single client. Plesk can be installed on a dedicated server to allow for the management and configuration of the server and websites through the Plesk control panel.

This glossary provides an overview of the main concepts and terms used in Plesk. With a deeper understanding of these terms, users will be able to more effectively use the Plesk management platform to efficiently and securely manage and configure servers and websites.

Index